JOHN THOMPSON'S
EASIEST PIANO COURSE

FIRST MOZART

Arranged by Christopher Hussey

ISBN 978-1-4950-6613-9

EXCLUSIVELY DISTRIBUTED BY

WILLIS MUSIC

HAL•LEONARD®
CORPORATION
7777 W. BLUEMOUND RD. P.O. BOX 13819
MILWAUKEE, WISCONSIN 53213

© 2016 by The Willis Music Co.
International Copyright Secured   All Rights Reserved

Visit Hal Leonard Online at
www.halleonard.com

Dies irae

Wolfgang Amadeus Mozart

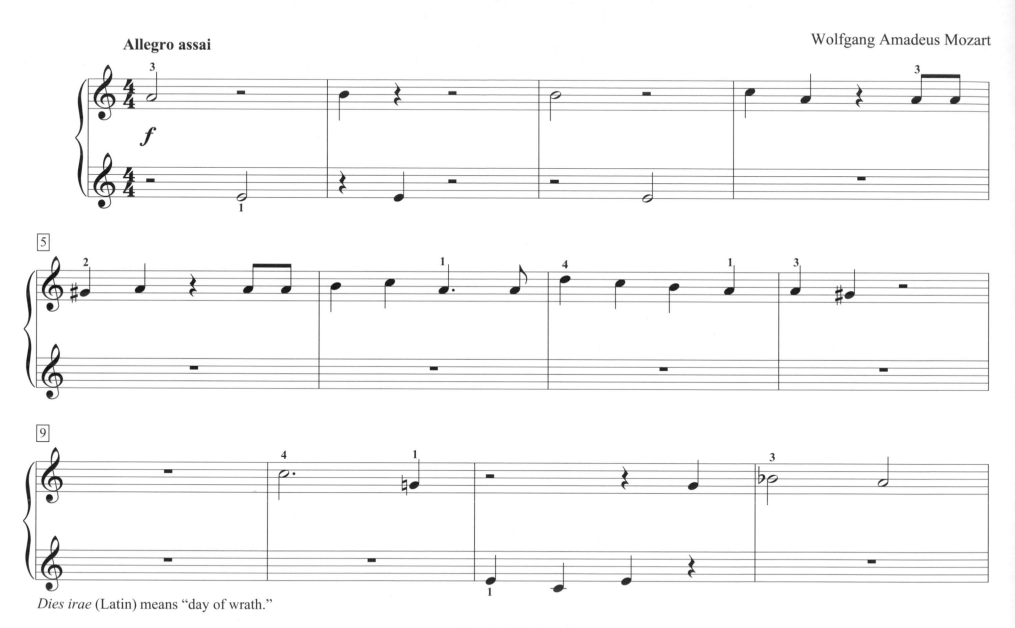

Dies irae (Latin) means "day of wrath."

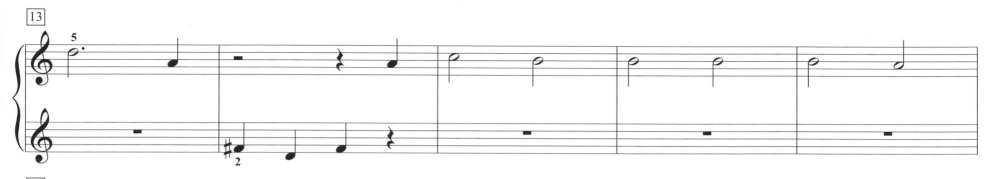

Ave verum corpus

Wolfgang Amadeus Mozart

Ave verum corpus (Latin) means "Hail, true body."

Là ci darem la mano

Wolfgang Amadeus Mozart

Là ci darem la mano (Italian) means "There we will give each other our hands."

Piano Sonata in C Major

Wolfgang Amadeus Mozart

Piano Concerto No. 21

Wolfgang Amadeus Mozart

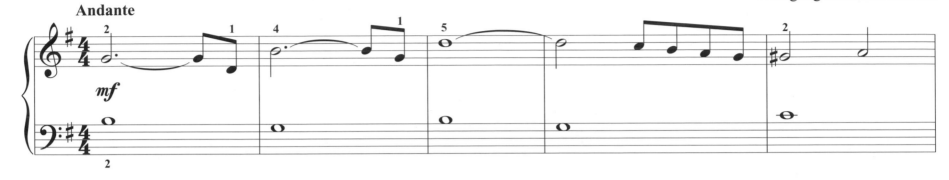

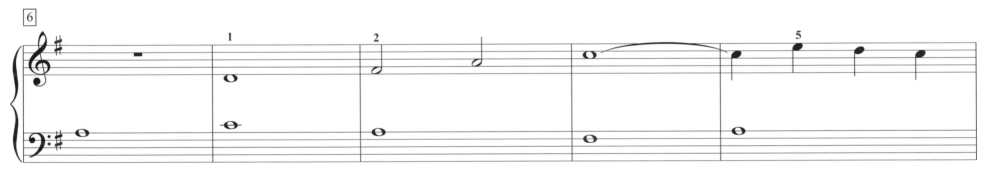

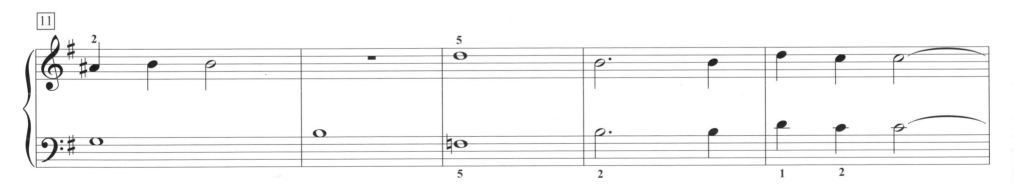

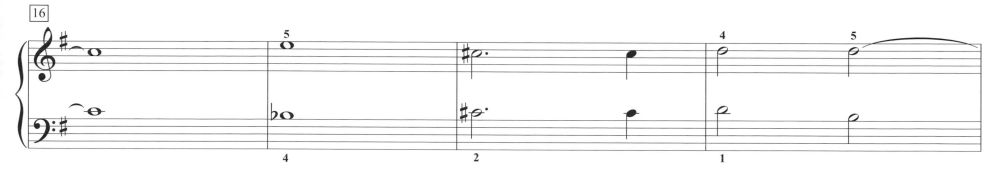

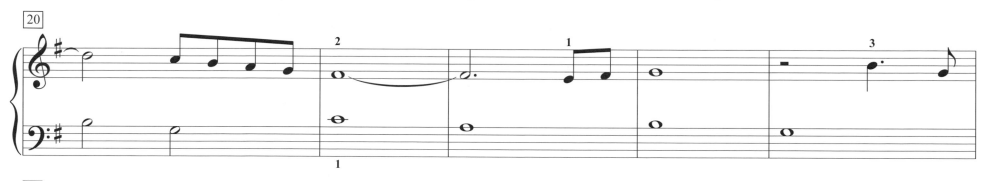

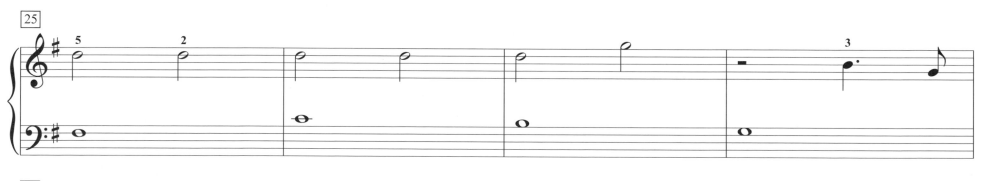

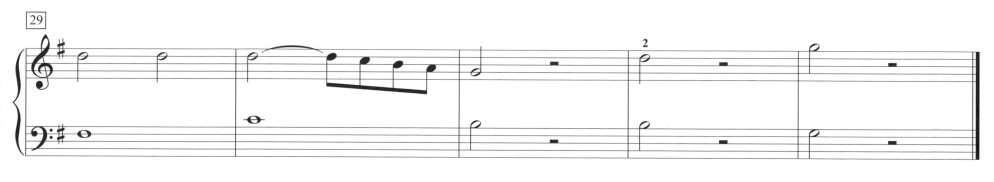

Symphony No. 40

Wolfgang Amadeus Mozart

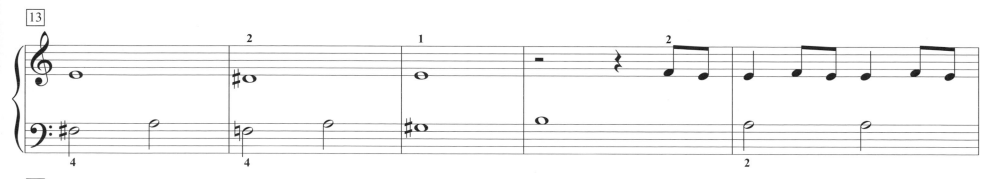

A Musical Joke

Wolfgang Amadeus Mozart

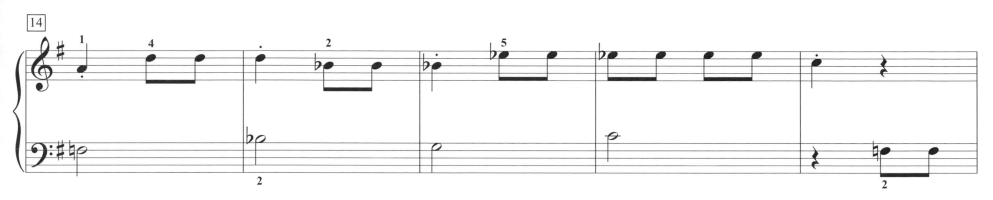

Horn Concerto No. 4

Wolfgang Amadeus Mozart

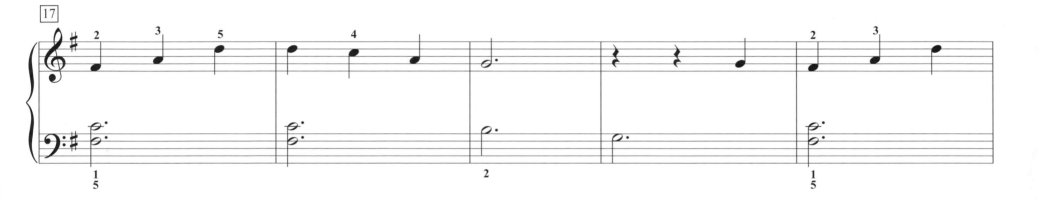

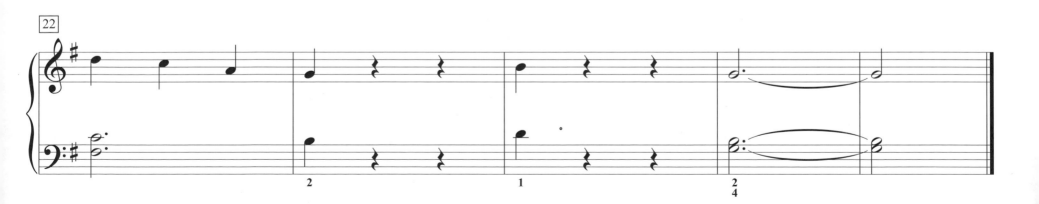

Clarinet Concerto

Wolfgang Amadeus Mozart

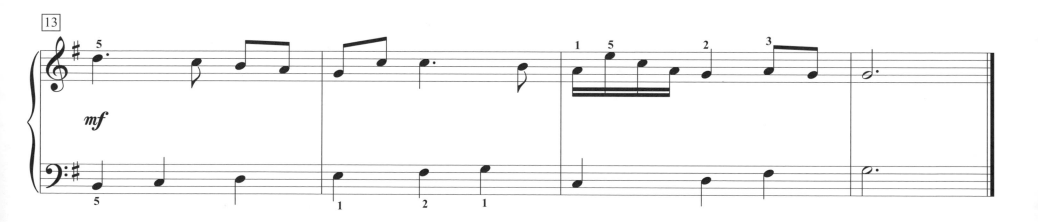

Piano Sonata No. 11

Wolfgang Amadeus Mozart

Andante grazioso

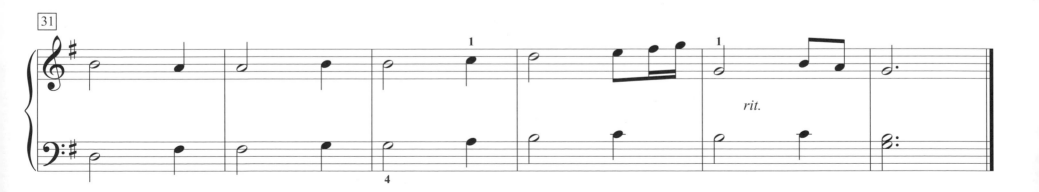

Minuet in F Major

Wolfgang Amadeus Mozart

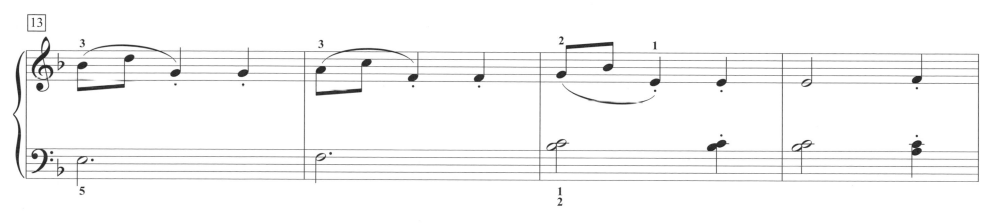

The Birdcatcher's Song

Wolfgang Amadeus Mozart

Andante

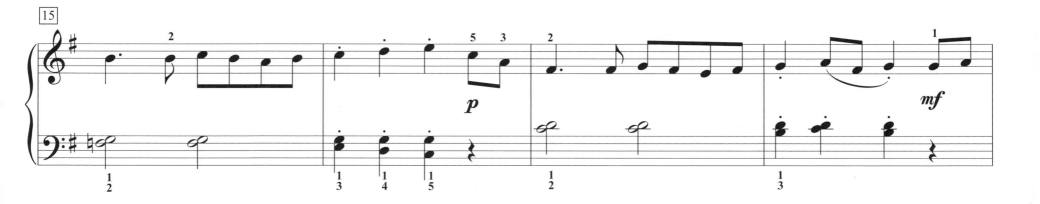

Eine kleine Nachtmusik

Wolfgang Amadeus Mozart

Eine kleine Nachtmusik (German) means "a little night music."

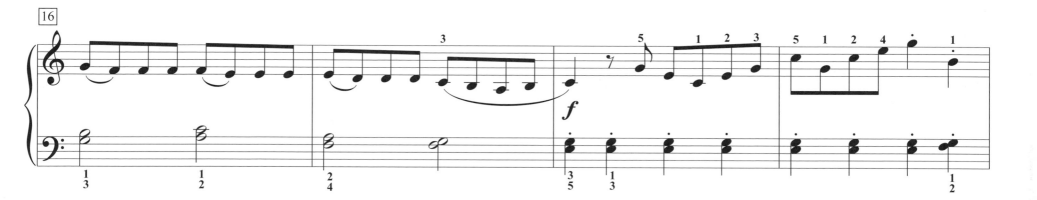

Non più andrai

Wolfgang Amadeus Mozart

Non più andrai (Italian) means "you shall go no more."

Gran Partita

Wolfgang Amadeus Mozart

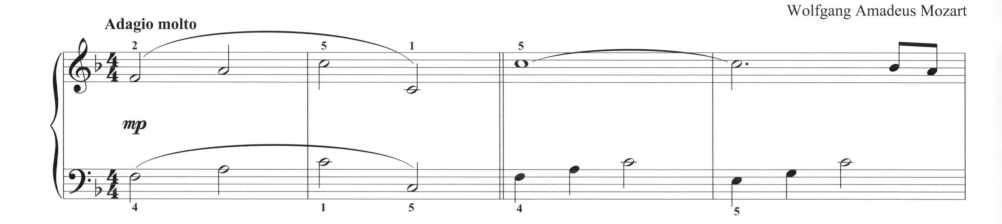

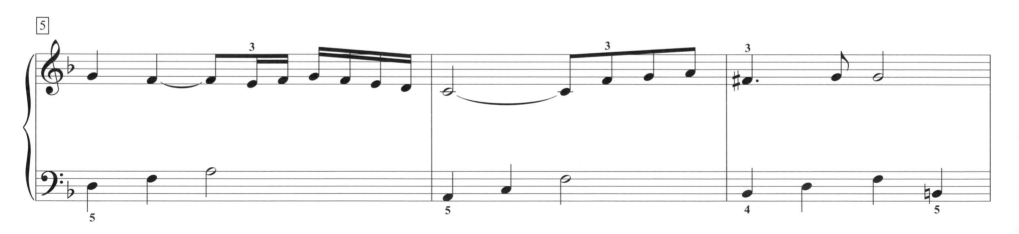

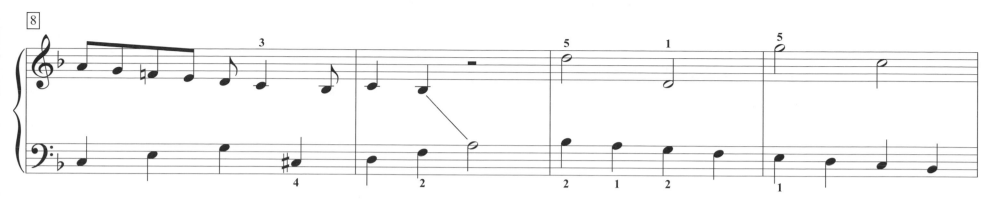

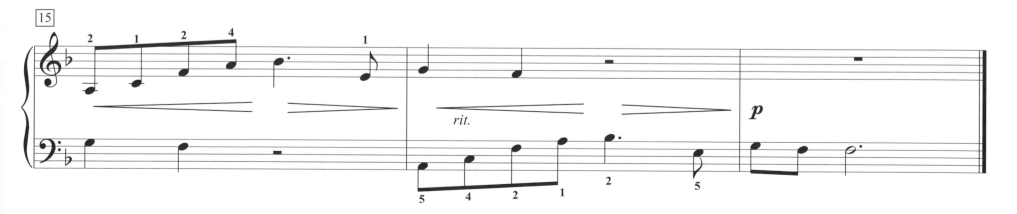

JOHN THOMPSON'S
EASIEST PIANO COURSE

Fun repertoire books are now available as an integral part of **John Thompson's Easiest Piano Course**. Graded to work alongside the course, these pieces are ideal for pupils reaching the end of the beginning level. They are invaluable for securing basic technique as well as developing musicality and enjoyment.

John Thompson's
Easiest Piano Course

00414014 Part 1 – Book only $5.99
00414018 Part 2 – Book only $6.99
00414019 Part 3 – Book only $6.99
00414112 Part 4 – Book only $6.99

First Christmas Duets

00416871...................................... $7.99

First Classics

00406347...................................... $5.99

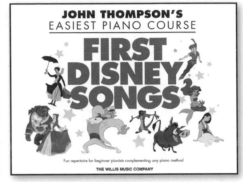

First Disney Songs

00416880.................................. $9.99

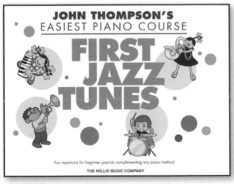

First Jazz Tunes

00120872...................................... $7.99

First Beethoven

00171709...................................... $7.99

First Chart Hits

00141171...................................... $7.99

EXCLUSIVELY DISTRIBUTED BY
HAL•LEONARD® CORPORATION
7777 W. BLUEMOUND RD. P.O. BOX 13819 MILWAUKEE, WI 53213

Also available:

First Christmas Tunes
00406426... $4.95

First Nursery Rhymes
00406229... $4.99

First Worship Songs
00416892... $8.99

Prices, contents and availability subject to change without notice.

Disney characters and artwork © Disney Enterprises Inc.

View complete songlists on **www.halleonard.com**